Samuel French Acting Edition

Monsoon Season

by Lizzie Vieh

SAMUELFRENCH.COM   SAMUELFRENCH.CO.UK

Copyright © 2020 by Lizzie Vieh
All Rights Reserved

MONSOON SEASON is fully protected under the copyright laws of the United States of America, the British Commonwealth, including Canada, and all member countries of the Berne Convention for the Protection of Literary and Artistic Works, the Universal Copyright Convention, and/or the World Trade Organization conforming to the Agreement on Trade Related Aspects of Intellectual Property Rights. All rights, including professional and amateur stage productions, recitation, lecturing, public reading, motion picture, radio broadcasting, television and the rights of translation into foreign languages are strictly reserved.

ISBN 978-0-573-70854-1

www.concordtheatricals.com
www.concordtheatricals.co.uk

FOR PRODUCTION ENQUIRIES

UNITED STATES AND CANADA
info@concordtheatricals.com
1-866-979-0447

UNITED KINGDOM AND EUROPE
licensing@concordtheatricals.co.uk
020-7054-7200

Each title is subject to availability from Concord Theatricals, depending upon country of performance. Please be aware that *MONSOON SEASON* may not be licensed by Concord Theatricals in your territory. Professional and amateur producers should contact the nearest Concord Theatricals office or licensing partner to verify availability.

CAUTION: Professional and amateur producers are hereby warned that *MONSOON SEASON* is subject to a licensing fee. Publication of this play(s) does not imply availability for performance. Both amateurs and professionals considering a production are strongly advised to apply to Concord Theatricalsbefore starting rehearsals, advertising, or booking a theater. A licensing fee must be paid whether the title(s) is presented for charity or gain and whether or not admission is charged. Professional/Stock licensing fees are quoted upon application to Concord Theatricals.

This work is published by Samuel French, an imprint of Concord Theatricals.

No one shall make any changes in this title(s) for the purpose of production. No part of this book may be reproduced, stored in a retrieval system, or transmitted in any form, by any means, now known or yet to be invented, including mechanical, electronic, photocopying, recording, videotaping, or otherwise, without the prior written permission of the publisher. No one shall upload this title(s), or part of this title(s), to any social media websites.

For all enquiries regarding motion picture, television, and other media rights, please contact Concord Theatricals.

MUSIC USE NOTE

Licensees are solely responsible for obtaining formal written permission from copyright owners to use copyrighted music in the performance of this play and are strongly cautioned to do so. If no such permission is obtained by the licensee, then the licensee must use only original music that the licensee owns and controls. Licensees are solely responsible and liable for all music clearances and shall indemnify the copyright owners of the play(s) and their licensing agent, Concord Theatricals, against any costs, expenses, losses and liabilities arising from the use of music by licensees. Please contact the appropriate music licensing authority in your territory for the rights to any incidental music.

IMPORTANT BILLING AND CREDIT REQUIREMENTS

If you have obtained performance rights to this title, please refer to your licensing agreement for important billing and credit requirements.

MONSOON SEASON was produced by All For One Theater at Underbelly at the Edinburgh Festival Fringe in August 2019. The production was directed by Kristin McCarthy Parker, with scenic design by You-Shin Chen, costume design by Haydee Zelideth, lighting design by Sarah Johnston, and sound design by Emma Wilk. The production stage manager was Kelly Burns. The cast was as follows:

DANNY...Richard Thieriot
JULIA ....Therese Plaehn

MONSOON SEASON was produced by All For One at Rattlestick Playwrights Theater in New York City in October 2019. The production was directed by Kristin McCarthy Parker, with scenic design by You-Shin Chen, costume design by Haydee Zelideth, lighting design by Sarah Johnston, and sound design by Emma Wilk. The production stage manager was Kara Kaufman, with assistant stage management by Andrea Jess Berkey and production management by Mae Frankeberger. The cast was as follows:

DANNY...Richard Thieriot
JULIA ....Therese Plaehn

A twenty-minute version of *MONSOON SEASON* was a finalist in the Samuel French Off Off Broadway Short Play Festival in 2016 at Classic Stage Company in New York City. The production was directed by Kristin McCarthy Parker. The cast was as follows:

DANNY...Richard Thieriot

CHARACTERS

DANNY – In his early forties. Recently divorced. Works for a technical support company in Phoenix, Arizona.

JULIA – In her late thirties. Recently divorced. Makeup artist. Wears a polished mask of makeup.

SETTING

Various locations in Phoenix, Arizona

TIME

Summer

AUTHOR'S NOTE

An asterisk (*) indicates Danny has entered a microsleep.

PART ONE - DANNY

DANNY. Julia got to keep the house.

We didn't want to uproot Samantha, and since Julia got to keep her too – Well, they live there now, and I don't.

I got my own apartment.

It's by the freeway on the edge of the mountain preserve. It's a motel-style rectangle centered around a shallow pool.

A strip club just opened next door. It's called Peaches. My bedroom window faces its parking lot.

It has a big neon sign. It's five peaches in an arc, kind of like one peach tossed through space in stop-animation.

They light up one at a time. It starts with the one on the left, a sort of soft salmon – then peach – then bright pink – then pinkish-red – then the last one – dark red. The red one holds for a few seconds – then the sequence starts over.

I don't have blinds yet.

So all night there's this wash of pink and red sweeping across my bedroom.

I'm not sleeping well.

*

Doctor Miller tells me they're called "microsleeps." A result of prolonged sleep deprivation. I don't know when I'm having them, but suddenly I'm veering off the side of the road or I've typed gibberish for half a page. She started to go into more clinical detail, but I zoned out.

*

*(**DANNY** is in his cubicle at work.)*

Hi, Jodi? I'm Danny, come on in.

How's your first day going? It gets easier.

We're cubicle buddies, so if you need anything, just pop your head over.

It's pretty simple really.

Memorize your scripts.

I mean, you can go off-script if you want. You're a human being. But you probably won't need to.

How about I take a few calls, let you listen, get a feel for what we do. Sound good?

(He puts on a phone headset and answers a call.)

Good afternoon, Southwest Network Solutions, this is Danny.

May I have your name?

That's Ann – A-N-N – Goodman – G-O-O-D-M-A-N – oh, Ann with an E – that's interesting.

And what seems to be the problem?

Your agents cannot make or receive any telephone calls. That is a problem, isn't it.

What kind of system do you have?

AmbiTrax500 – uh-oh, not the AmbiTrax. If I had a nickel for every – Time *is* money, I've heard that.

Have you tried turning the system off and turning it on again?

I have to ask. It's the Miranda Rights of technical support.

I'm going to have to ask you to do it again.

I'll wait.

(Brief pause.)

It's working...? Well there we go! Isn't that – Hello? ...Anne?

(Loud thunk – a bird flies into the window.)

It's okay. It's just a bird. It's a glass building – they fly into it all the time.

Especially during monsoon season. Heat lightning, electrical storms – they go berserk, like kamikaze pilots, they just...

> *(He gestures a plane hitting an object and exploding.)*

*

*(**DANNY** is browsing at a pet store.)*

I don't know, my daughter keeps begging for a cat, and my wife won't get her one, so I thought hey there's something I can do to make Dad's house better, get her a pet, you know?

No, not an actual cat, cats hate me. I dunno. A fish or something?

No kid wants a fish.

Oh. Whoa. Look at these guys. These...hermit crabs?

They are going at it. They are...killing each other, that is brutal.

Why don't you put another shell in there so they don't have to fight over the same one?

Fun to watch. Guess it is that.

(Pause.)

Look at that poor little guy. That big guy is gonna destroy him. He doesn't stand a chance.

Jesus, he's gonna kill him, come on, get him out of there –

I'll take him.

*

(**DANNY** *is driving an Uber.*)

Pam?

Oh good, if you weren't Pam, I'd have to yell, "Help! Some insane woman is getting in my car!"

(He adjusts the radio.)

You hear about this? Juárez Cartel? Police found a bunch of garbage bags full of body parts in an abandoned strip mall. All the heads removed. Hands too, so no fingerprints. Smart, right?

Yeah, I can change it.

Uhh... I got a book on tape?

It's "Who Moved My Cheese?" Narrated by the man himself, Tony Robbins.[*]

Far as I can tell, it's about these people stuck in a rat maze, and some sadistic monster keeps moving their cheese around, so they're starving to death.

Reminds me of that movie *Saw*.

I know, and they call this "self-help"?

I'm a sucker, I read the box and it says, "It's fast, it's simple, and it works!"

Ha, more like, "It's slow, it's complicated, and you're driving an Uber to cover child support!" Your... headphones are on. Okay.

"It is safer to search in the maze than to remain in a cheeseless situation." Oof. Feel that.

(Pause.)

Well, this old rat is *trying* to learn new tricks, but it don't come easy...

(Pause.)

...But the cheese used to be there! It was there every time! Someone moved it! Who?!

Whoa! Didn't mean to swerve there... Sorry.

*

---

[*]A license to produce *Monsoon Season* does not include a performance license for any third-party or copyrighted recordings. Licensees should create their own.

>   (**DANNY** *is with his mom at a nursing home.*)

How's the Ensure?

No, you drink it Mom, I eat all the time. I had… birthday cake for lunch, some gal at work, it was her fiftieth, we all –

Oh – that's – right in your lap – you got paper towels in here? It's fine Mom, I got it.

>   (*He cleans up the spilled Ensure with paper towels and disposes of them in a waste basket. He ties up the trash bag to remove later.*)

They ever take out your trash around here?

Who feeds me? I feed me. No, we're separated. Remember? I moved out. She's on to "bigger and better things."

It's not Stephen, Mom, it's Danny. Danny. Stephen's in Miami with his family. Uh-huh. That's right, they have the big house right on the water. Yup, and I'm the one getting divorced, that's right.

Why don't I have a house on the beach? 'Cause we live in a fu– 'cause we live in a desert.

Here's a way to keep us straight. Stephen's the one who hasn't visited in four years, and I'm the one who comes every week. You got that, Mom?

>   (*Pause.*)

I'll take you out on the boat soon. Miami's great. Humid, but great.

*

(**DANNY** *is on his cell phone in the Peaches parking lot. He is drunk.*)

I was only twenty minutes late, Jules.

I understand that's a long time to a four-year-old, but I left with plenty of –

There was an accident on the 101, it was gridlock –

I haven't seen her in over two weeks –

You know last time I went to hug her she pulled away? Like she didn't know me?

Do you know what that does to me?

That's a knife in my guts.

Yeah, a little.

I was angry, I was upset, I went to a bar.

I'm in the parking lot.

I'm *not* driving home, it's next door to my apartment.

Did I have dinner...? Why do you *care*?

Why *should* I eat?

Why should I sleep?

Why should I get out of bed?

I love you.

So what. It's true.

I'll do anything.

(He listens.)

(His face changes.)

Whoa whoa whoa...

What guy?

Shane? That guy who fixed the screen door?

That's not how you introduced him, you never said...

No. No.

That is not allowed. I do not allow that.

I will... I will evict him.

I will come over. I will remove him.

I will drag him out of my house and pop his skull like a fucking grape.

He does not get to live in my house.
He does not get to live with my family.
Julia...? Julia?

>   *(His nose starts to bleed.)*

*

(**DANNY** *is at Peaches. It's loud.*)

Chrissy, that's a pretty name, is that short for Christine? Christina, nice, even better.

You girls worked here long? I said, have you – can you hear anything in here? You're young, how old are you anyway?

Summer I was twenty-two, I worked construction and me and my buddy Mike Lippinlaw went to the gym every night after work. I could bench-press one-sixty back then.

One-sixty.

One. Sixty.

It's pretty good.

It's not bad.

It's okay.

You girls working late tonight? Doing anything after?

I said are you working late, maybe you wanna do anything after?

I said are you –

I said I keep having a nightmare where my wife tosses me a water balloon full of blood.

I haven't had sex in eight months.

I didn't say anything.

*

(**DANNY** *is at home, with Sammy.*)

Sammy, come look. Your bedroom's gonna be right in there, and here's where we can watch TV, and once Daddy gets a table we can eat dinner right here.

This is kinda fun, you wanna help Daddy with this?

(*He picks up scissors.*)

This window is so big, and it's so bright at night, so I've been cutting up these newspapers and magazines and taping them up here. That way I can sleep at night. It's like making a collage, you wanna...?

Hey Sammy. Guess what Daddy got you. I got you a pet.

No, not a kitty. Not a puppy. It's a hermit crab.

A hermit crab. Well, he's right in here silly, he's inside his shell. See? He's right there, that's his claw.

He's hiding right now. Maybe he's sleeping. He'll come out. You just gotta wait, he's very shy Sammy.

So...we watch him. We sit, and we watch him. And we wait. For him to...do something.

(*Pause.*)

Well, maybe a kitty would be more fun, but you don't get a kitty, 'cause you already have a hermit crab. Mommy would not say you could have a kitty, maybe if Mommy would answer my phone calls, then maybe – Daddy? No, I'm your daddy. Sammy. I'm your dad. Did he – did *Shane* tell you to call him that? 'Cause he's no one – I googled him – he's not anyone, he's –

*

> (**DANNY** *is at work, wearing his headset. He's on his computer. He finds a phone number online.*)

Thank you, public records.

> (*He dials a number and uses a voice modulator.*)

Hola, Shane.

I'm watching you, pendejo.

Don't mess with Juárez.

Clear out of this neighborhood, or they'll find your head in a garbage bag. Every time you take a breath, it's because I am allowing you to take that breath, and every –

*

*(**DANNY** is with his mom at the nursing home.)*

I don't know, Mom. I can't answer that. You'd have to ask her, she's the one who wanted to "change her life." No, she didn't – find someone else – there's reasons – there's other reasons it doesn't work out sometimes, it's not like – Hit her? Jesus Mom, no –

Well Dad did beat the shit out of you, and you didn't leave, so I guess your little theory doesn't –

Fuck. I'm sorry. I didn't mean to – Oh God, your –

Can I get some help? There's something wrong with her – something with her tube –

Yeah, take her. Bye Mom. I'll be back next –

*

> (**DANNY** *runs after a traffic cop. At some point during this scene a car alarm starts going off.*)

Please, officer, I was only in there two minutes, I just had to pick up my laundry, all my shirts are covered in –

No, I'm not handicapped. I know there's no excuse, I just –

Look, I cannot afford $150 right now. I can't afford blinds. I'm eating Del Taco every meal, my nose is leaking like a goddamn faucet –

Please.

Please, ma'am, I am begging you.

> (*He kneels.*)

I am on my knees.

As one human being to another – can you PLEASE just –

*

(Blackout. Car alarm grows louder.)
(Lights up on **DANNY** *holding scissors.)*
What am I doing with these...
(He laughs.)
Oh she's gonna love this.

*

(**DANNY** *is at his apartment, talking to Julia.*)

Yeah, it is a mess, that's what happens when you just drop in –

It's a burst blood vessel or something – Look, it's fine Jules, I don't need –

Please don't touch me. Just – don't.

(*Pause.*)

What did you want to talk about?

Why do you just assume it's me calling him?

I mean – I bet all sorts of people wanna hurt him. I do.

Did I cut a hole in your screen door?

That's insane, why would I do that.

No, I'm not sneaking into your backyard, I'm not a maniac.

You know what, that's enough, it's time for you to go. Oh, you know what –

(*He gets a box full of stuff.*)

I have a box for you, some clothes, your face-scrubby thing, our wedding album – shit I'll throw it out if you don't want it.

(*Pause.*)

I'm not full of hate.

I miss you too.

Without you – I'm lost – I can't – nothing matters...

Can we pretend all this has been a nightmare? I promise you. I can be different.

(*Long pause.*)

Don't bother. Just leave. And Julia –

(*He grabs a trash bag and piles her stuff into it.*)

Take your trash, I'm done cleaning up after you.

(*He hurls the bag out the door.*)

*

*(**DANNY** is outside Peaches.)*

I didn't hurt her, I just touched her arm – could you – please, just let me back in, it's not a big deal, I'm not gonna – *God...*

You are the biggest fucking man I've ever seen, what do you weigh, 350? 400 pounds?

I bet everyone thinks you're so tough but maybe you're not, maybe you're not tough at all, and you know the only thing worse than being a guy who looks like a big tough motherfucker but who's actually weak and vulnerable? It's being a guy who looks weak and vulnerable and actually is weak and vulnerable.

And the funny part is, in another world, maybe you and me coulda been friends. Me, you, and your big bald head. But it's too late now. We're too far down this path –

If I charged you right now would you have to kill me?

*

(**DANNY** *is at home with his hermit crab. He's drunk and disheveled. There's an unopened envelope next to him.*)

You are the worst fucking pet.

I come anywhere near you, you just hide in your fucking shell. Like a little fucking bitch.

Why do you hate me?

I never even gave you a name.

I thought Sammy would.

If Sammy was a boy, I wanted to name her Brian.

Julia said no, I don't like the name Brian, we'll do Samuel if it's a boy and Samantha if it's a girl, and I said why do our options have to be boy/girl versions of the same name and she said so either way we can call it Sammy and I said so what you mean is either way you get what you want and she said stop being an asshole so I went out and got drunk and she was pissed so then I tried to put the crib together as a peace gesture 'cause she'd been nagging me to do it for weeks so I tried but I was drunk and I broke one of the legs and she cried and I slept in the car.

(*He opens the envelope with scissors.*)

"Temporary order for protection against stalking, aggravated stalking or harassment."

What did I ever do to you?

I did the best I could so why do you fucking hate me?

*

(**DANNY** *is at work. He is squeezing a stress ball.*)

You say "terrorizing," Jason, like I was setting out to scare her, like Jodi herself expressed no interest in the story, when it was Jodi herself who kept bringing up the corpse without a head, when it was Jodi herself who used the word "head" up to fourteen times in under twenty minutes – I counted, I counted Jason – and I ask you, is that the behavior of a healthy human being? Is that a pure soul, sitting there in her cubicle saying "head" to me over and over and *over* like some witch crone in a fairy tale? And yet I'm the one getting chewed out, and Jodi herself sits riding a cloud of cotton candy over there, raving about decapitated heads, and she says I stole *her* stress ball? Who is the one under stress here? Jodi the evil headless witch, or me, the poor guy trapped next to her and you're goddamn right I took her stress ball because squeezing this ball is the only thing keeping my body from tumbling headless into the abyss and there is no need to *fire* me Jason, because I am already burning, burning, burning –

*

*(**DANNY** crouches in the driveway of his old house.)*

That's why Mommy doesn't want you to see me, 'cause she doesn't want you to be scared. But you're not scared. It's just Dad. Sammy's not scared.

Pink chalk! That's the best chalk! What'd you draw?

I can see from here, I like it here by the garbage can, it's so hot out, I wanna stay in the shade.

It's a kitty cat! And it's eating a...hermit crab...

Sammy. Come here. I need you to listen, 'cause your mom or – or – might look outside, and –

Come here.

We used to get ice cream on Sundays but now your mom is – your mom and *Shane* are...the point is, even if I'm not around, you gotta know that it's not because I – it's not about you, and it's never 'cause I don't love you as absolutely much as it is possible for a dad to love, 'cause I do, it's just that – um – your dad's been –

He's looking. Run inside. Go.

*

> (**DANNY** *hides in Julia's backyard. He watches her through the window.*)

Ever hear of blinds?
Anyone could see you right now.
Any psycho in your yard.
Think you can cut me out of your life?
Snip snip?
Think your little boy toy can fix everything, he can protect you?
I will cut my way back in, Julia.

> (*He moves toward the house, brandishing scissors.*)
>
> (*Rumble of thunder.*)

*

*(**DANNY** is in line at Home Depot. He holds a large box. He chats with the person near him in line.)*

Doin' some painting?

I like that color.

I like green.

It's very soothing, like you're in a forest, or a jungle, or inside a lava lamp –

Wife picked it out? The old ball and chain.

Women – can't live with 'em, can't – Oh –

(It's his turn at the counter.)

Yeah hi, I just want to make sure – I bought the Echo fourteen-inch Gas Two-Stroke chainsaw earlier, and I think I need to upgrade to the twenty-inch here, but I wanna make sure it's up to the job –

Well – there's this uh, cactus in my yard, it's – it's fucking huge, is what it is, and, well – dead, so I'm cutting it down, and then I need to cut it into smaller pieces so I can cart it away, and the fourteen-inch kept *sticking*, you know? I basically destroyed it, had to throw it away.

Anyway – think this bad boy will do the trick?

*

(**DANNY** *is driving an Uber.*)

You like that song, Capitan?

When I was your age, I would drive my car around and BLAST that song, you know?

Well, next year. When you get your license. You'll see.

You like skeletons?

You have a skeleton on your t-shirt.

See that old shopping center?

You hear what the Juárez Cartel is doing?

They're hiding bodies in old strip malls.

All chopped up, different parts in different garbage bags.

Last week they found one in an old Linens 'n Things.

No head.

Gone.

Know what I think though?

That head'll show up.

This dry climate – it's not gonna decompose.

Phoenix is a lot like Ancient Egypt. The dry air – it's why mummies are so well preserved.

Can't leave a head just anywhere.

Know what I mean?

Gotta get creative.

*

(It's raining. **DANNY** *is asleep at his apartment. He wakes up and looks at his phone.)*

Whoa.

How long was I...sixteen hours?!

(Laughs.) I feel *great*.

> *(Pause.)*

Just one last thing, Danny.

*

*(**DANNY** is behind Peaches. Thunder and lightning. He holds something.)*

Imagine a basketball...not heavy enough...a basketball full of sand. It's wrapped in plastic bags. Monsoon season, it's pouring, there's a flash flood in the ravine behind the strip club. A dry ditch is now a raging river. It's dark, but there's flashes of pink and red from the neon sign. You hold it. You feel its weight. Take it in so you can forget it forever. Then – toss. It arcs in slow motion – stop-animation like a peach. Like a grape. Pink. Peach. Red. Hold at red. Splash. Gone.

*

PART TWO - JULIA

1.

JULIA. I got to keep the house.

Obviously.

People tend to like Danny better.

Fine, like him better, fuck you.

You never had to live with him.

He picked our wedding song. Michael Bolton, "When a Man Loves a Woman." I'm like – Great, Danny. A song all about how *you* feel.

I met him at a bar.

He played in a cover band every Tuesday night. The Doors.

The first time I saw him he was playing keyboard on "People Are Strange," which might sound sexy, if you like The Doors, but I don't. They fucking suck.

I got drunk and had sex with him.

That would have been that, but the thing about Danny is...he grows on you. Like a fungus.

Like a barnacle.

Seems harmless at first, until the day you wake up almost forty and realize that he is *feeding* off you.

One night I was in line at the pharmacy and all of a sudden I saw myself in the mirror behind the counter – and I thought, "Who is that – old – poor – *ugly* woman?"

That can't be me.

I don't care what it takes, if I have to give up sleeping, if the Adderall makes my hands shake like a vibrator –

'Cause bottom line, I'd rather kill myself than wind up like that poor slob in the mirror.

Is that off-putting?

I hate that you need people to like you to get what you want.

It's insulting.

But I *want* to get what I want. So –

> *(She flashes a huge Miss America smile.)*

Pretty good, right?

(Mutters.) Fuck me.

2.

> (**JULIA** *is filming herself at home for a YouTube makeup tutorial. Throughout this video she struggles with shaking hands.*)

Whatsup guys, it's Julia, and this is Pretty as Fuck!
To our 524 brand-new subscribers this week – welcome to Part Four of our Summer Transformation Series!
Today I've got a special treat for you guys – we have a new corporate sponsor, and I cannot *wait* to try out this product.

> (*She pulls out a bizarre-looking metal contraption that looks kind of like a vibrator.*)

Say hello to the –

> (*She drops the device.*)

Shit! …Fuck, did I…? – It's fine –
Say hello to the 4EvaYoung VitaMask 3000, the latest in Korean at-home face-lift technology.
This skin-tightening device releases 30,000 microamps of electric current, rapidly tightening and releasing the muscles of the face.
Guys, I'm so excited about this thing.
I just got it in the mail yesterday, this is the talk on all the beauty blogs… I can't wait to try it out.
I've been letting this guy charge, it's set to "maximum tightening"…we are ready to roll.

> (*She turns the device on and applies it to her face.*)

OH MY FUCKING GOD!

> (*She drops/throws the device.*)

Whoa.
Wow.
I did not expect it to hurt that much.

Umm...okay, lemme look at the instructions...

Okay, my bad, it says to set it to whatever level you can bear – I must have had it on too high, let's try this again...

> *(She puts it back on her face. She grimaces but leaves it there.)*

Okay!

Here we go.

We're doing it.

This is happening.

...I feel like I'm being electrocuted.

It's like my muscles are...out of control...like tiny little people are grabbing them, and jiggling them back and forth *really* fast!

> *(She bravely endures a few more moments of the device.)*

And that's it!

Just twenty minutes of that, twice a day, for a month!

You can get a fifteen percent discount on the 4EvaYoung VitaMask by using promo code JULIAFACE.

> *(She poses with the device and accidentally drops it again.)*

– Fuck –

3.

> (**JULIA** *is at a dive bar, where her friend Paula works.*)

Yeah, gimme another vodka/Diet Coke...

Is it just me, or did there used to be more men at this bar?

I don't know, it felt like back when we were in beauty school, there'd always be hot guys here.

Now they're all...twelve, or short, or poor.

Like why did I even bother with the push-up bra, girls these days don't even wear bras, they wear, like "bralettes," it's bullshit.

We're *not* old Paula, we're hot as fuck.

God, we used to *rule* this bar.

> (*Pause. She looks around. There's no one of interest.*)

I worry I wasted my hot years on Danny.

> (*She washes down an Adderall with her cocktail. She sees someone.*)

Paula. PaulaPaulaPaula. Nine o'clock. No *your* nine o'clock, the guy coming out of the back room, he's leaving, he's leaving – fuck, Paula, you know him?

Shane?

I've never seen him in here before.

He can't be a handyman, he's getting into a BMW...

Ha, that makes more sense.

You have his number?

Gimme his card, I'll call and say I need a handyman.

4.

>(**JULIA** *is at home with Shane.*)
>
>(*She watches him work and holds his hammer.*)

That is amazing.

My ex-husband fiddled with that light fixture for *months* and couldn't fix it.

You come over, you don't even need this, just BAM – two minutes, it's done.

Um...you fixed everything so fast, this took way less time than I thought...

Oh yeah! The screen door over here, there's this big hole in it?

It almost looks like someone cut it.

I kinda think my ex-husband might be fucking with me?

Ha, no, he's not dangerous, he's just a loser.

Think you can fix it?

>(*She gets closer to him.*)

Can I see your tattoo?

Ooh, it's kinda scary-looking, is that a...bird?

Oh, cool, a...plague doctor...

(*Reads.*) "Life Is Contagion."

That's so true.

...So what do you do when you're not handy-manning?

Yeah, Paula mentioned that...

You sell Adderall?

Yeah, I'd definitely be interested.

Maybe I'd be interested in that too.

Tonight might work, what time is it?

>(*She laughs.*)

No, I'm sorry, I'm not laughing at you, it's just...that is the biggest fucking Rolex I have ever seen.

I love it.

5.

*(**JULIA** is at home with her mom, late at night.)*

I know I said midnight, my Uber Pool took for fucking ever.

Mom...will you chill out? You're gonna wake up Sammy. God, it reeks in here. How many Virginia Slims did you smoke?

K, you know what, Mom?

Look.

Right here.

This is who I went out with.

(She shows her mom a picture on her phone.)

Shane. I told you – the handyman? Paula's friend? 6'4".

Uh yeah, he works out.

Oh it's real, I checked it out, the logos are legit.

And – you'll love this – he smokes!

Mom – this guy is the real deal. He's the opposite of Danny.

He's got money, he's confident, he knows what he wants.

You think I don't *know* how hard it is to find a man when you got a kid?

Who are you to give me advice?

I have one ex-husband.

You have four.

Maybe I should just do what you'd do: marry him after knowing him a month, and then stay with him even if he throws a hair dryer at my daughter's face.

My knuckle still doesn't straighten all the way, you know, so thanks for that.

(Pause.)

I'm not rushing into anything. I just like him.

Yeah, she misses him, but I'm doing this for her too.

I mean, what kind of example was Danny setting?

(She jumps up, startled.)

Oh my God...!

I just – saw my reflection in the window, I thought there was someone outside –

I'm sorry, it really startled me.

I get nervous living alone, I can't help it.

6.

(JULIA *crouches next to Sammy's bed.*)

Sammy.
You need to come out from under there, honey.
I can't fit under your bed.
Why are you so scared of a bird?
Birds aren't scary.
What show were you watching?
...Okay.
That's not something Shane should have let you watch. That's not for kids.
Those birds, what are they called?
The Marabou stork?
We don't have those in Arizona. They live in – that's right, Africa, they can't fly over here.
Well...if they eat dead animals, that means they don't eat people!
So it's actually a good thing, right?

(*She stands and looks out the window.*)

Okay, I'm looking.
By the gate? That's our barbeque.
Behind that's an umbrella.
I promise. No birds. Nothing.

(*Pause.*)

I know you wish Daddy was here to scare it away.
He's coming by Sunday to take you out for ice cream –

(*Pause.*)

You wanna do finger paints?
You wanna organize Shane's hammers?
You wanna do chalk in the driveway?
I can't just invite Daddy over, sweetheart...it doesn't work like that.
You're breaking my heart.
Okay. I'll go.

7.

>(**JULIA** *is outside a client's house. On the phone. Sammy is nearby.*)

Only twenty minutes?

She's four, Danny, she was crying, she thought everyone forgot her.

And it was forty-five minutes.

The school called me 'cause all the other kids were picked up, it was just her and Miss Tanya sitting there, waiting.

Hell no, you are not picking her up now, I've got a house full of rich high-school girls waiting for me, I'm not having my creepy ex-husband show up.

Sammy, I'm *using* the phone, you can't watch Baby Shark right now –

Stop.

Stop.

Play by the golf cart.

Have you been drinking?

That doesn't mean I automatically stop caring about you, I –

>(*Pause.*)

...Don't do this, I –

I can't talk about this right now, I'm –

Fine, you wanna know?

There is someone else.

Shane.

You met him.

You came to pick up Sammy, he was working on the –

I don't know. Two months? Three?

He's moving in.

To the house, he's moving in.

Fuck you, I need *money* Danny.

Maybe If you were paying your child support, maybe I wouldn't have to take in a *tenant*, Danny, maybe –
Go fuck yourself.

>*(She hangs up the phone.)*

No, I'm sorry sweetie.
Come here. I'm not mad at you.
Mama's gonna put makeup on lots of pretty girls, and you're gonna be my helper, okay?
You run inside, tell them I'm coming.
I gotta get my bags.

>*(Sammy runs inside.)*

God, I need to get fucked up.

>*(She takes several Adderall.)*

8.

> (**JULIA** *is passed out. Her phone rings a bunch of times. She doesn't move. Finally, she picks up, groggy and out of it.*)

Hello?

"Birdman"?

Ugh...how'd you get this number, this isn't Birdman, this is his girlfriend –

If he said he'd call you Saturday about some coke, then he'll call you.

Well, it's not Saturday, it's –

Fuckfuckfuckfuckfuckfuckfuckfuck –

What's the date?

Nonononononononononono...

> (*She hangs up, panicking.*)

Shane! Shane!

> (*Shane enters.*)

Did you turn off my alarm?

FUCK, why didn't you wake me up?

I had an appointment this morning.

A wedding. I was supposed to do makeup for the bride...

Oh God.

This is bad. This is really, really bad...

Will you call her?

Pretend you're the hospital – say I'm in the emergency room – I got hit by a car!

I didn't mean to! We were out 'til like three last night –

If this gets out, no one will ever hire me again.

'Cause I don't want to rely on you for all my money is why.

'Cause then what am I, a hooker?

I'm not "taking a tone," I'm talking to you, is that *allowed*?

> (*Shane throws a plate against the wall.*)

JESUS you gonna throw a plate every time I say something you don't like?
I've already lived in a trailer park hon, I don't need to –
If you throw that at me, I swear to God, I'll –

9.

> (**JULIA** *is at Paula's bar, drinking alone. She notices a stranger a few seats away.*)

Take a picture, it'll last longer.
I just...noticed you looking at me.
It's fine, it doesn't bother me, just thought I'd acknowledge.
Be my guest.

> (*He comes closer.*)

Nope, not waiting for anyone. Just...little old me. (*Laughs flirtatiously.*) ...What?
Oh.
Yeah. Um...
I can scoot over.
You know what?
You can have all the seats.
I'm done.

> (*She quickly drains her drink in a few big gulps and stands.*)

By the way, your watch?
Pretty obvious fake.
Tacky.
Tacky!

> (*She leaves.*)

10.

(JULIA gets ready for bed.)

What's this show?

There's a lotta cops.

Oh.

C-O-P-S.

I didn't know it was still on the air.

(Long pause. She fidgets.)

So.

It's been two days, are you gonna not talk to me forever?

I'm not trying to start something, I just – why are you still so mad?

(Pause.)

Oh God, he's still calling you? I told him –

No – don't call your boys, don't do anything.

Shane, please, will you calm down?

Just leave him alone, I can handle Danny, I'll make him stop.

Please? Will you let me handle it?

(Pause.)

Is there anything I can do to make all this up to you?

Oooh.

I could be into that.

Well…it's not something I like *all* the time, but…you know, sometimes. When the mood strikes.

Yeah, you go pee. I'll get ready.

(Shane leaves the room.)

(JULIA takes several Adderall.)

11.

>(**JULIA** *is creating a YouTube video.*)

Strap on your seatbelts kids.

I am not fucking around today.

Today. We contour.

For the uninitiated – contouring is using several different shades of foundation to create contour in the face where it does not naturally exist.

When I was pregnant with my daughter I gained thirty pounds and my face looked like a balloon. I learned to contour – BAM – jawline.

No, you know what? It goes back further.

When I was seventeen I wanted a job doing makeup, but there just wasn't much of a market for that in shithole Corpus Christi.

But you know what job I did get?

Putting makeup on dead people.

Not kidding. First job. God, it was gross.

Though sometimes, when I'm doing eye-makeup on a real twitcher and they just WON'T HOLD STILL, I miss the corpses.

They never moved.

Like giant birds, laid out on a table...

>(*Pause.*)

I shouldn't post this.

I'm Too High to YouTube.

That should be the name of a country song. Is it already?

So a lot of you objected to my use of the term "crack whore" in my last post, but, to be fair, a crack whore is a person who fucks people – for drugs!

So...how am I *not* a crack whore?

I mean – I'd probably have sex with Shane anyway, he's hot, but shit, I pretend all day, I don't wanna fucking *role play* in bed, I'm not an elf, I'm not a...Biblical concubine. Grow up.

I am ashamed though. I'm very ashamed.
> *(Notices something outside.)*

Is there someone in my fucking yard?

12.

>   (**JULIA** *is at Danny's apartment.*)

Your place looks like shit.

What's wrong with your nose?

You have blood on your – no, it's – let me –

Fine, I'm not touching you.

>   (*Pause.*)

You gotta stop calling Shane.

Oh please, we know it's you –

This is serious, do you know what he wants to do to you?

Were you in my yard last night?

Well *someone* cut the fucking screen door open again, and I found *these*.

>   (*She pulls out a pair of scissors labelled "Danny."*)

Before you even – they say "Danny" on them.

I'm not afraid to get a restraining order. I know how, I looked online.

What are you doing – What is all this – Is this – what did you do to our wedding album? You cut out my face – in every single – Are you psycho?

You are so full of hate.

You think this is easy for me?

You think I don't miss you?

This has been a nightmare, it's not like I'm having a great time over here, it's not like I'm *happy* – my asshole hurts, I had to buy new plates, Sammy is practically *living* at my mom's.

>   (*Long pause.*)

I can't…it's not like…

No, I don't love him. I don't even know if I like him.

>   (*Pause.*)

How would that even work?
Look at your place. Look at your face.
Nothing's changed.
Fine, I'll go.

    (She heads to the door.)

What?
I don't *need* you to clean up after me, I don't need you for anything!

13.

> (**JULIA** *is at home, late at night. Paula arrives.*)

Thanks for coming, I know it's late, but I thought maybe you'd just be closing the bar? Good old Paula.

Um, I woke up at two a.m. and thought there was a giant bird looming over me.

I screamed my head off.

No one heard.

He's at the casino, Sammy's at my mom's.

So I've just been awake. Thinking and pacing. Pacing, and thinking.

> (*Pause.*)

Remember beauty school?

It was fun being roomies, wasn't it?

What if – you moved in here?

Well, see, I think I have to make Shane move out – he hit me – but I don't think he's gonna take that very well?

So I was thinking, don't live alone, 'cause like, people keep *showing up* in my backyard asking for drugs and looking for Shane, and – I've never lived alone, I don't like it –

It's not insane, I've given this a lot of thought.

I'm sorry it's not "clean" enough for you Paula, what, you think I have a maid?

Fine. You don't want to live with me, you've made that very clear.

Paula. Can I ask you a really serious question?

> (*Pause.*)

Will you demonstrate the VitaMask for my viewers?

My sponsors are gonna pull out if I don't do a new video, they said it has to be normal.

Please?

Please, Paula?

Paula, PLEASE.
PLEASE. PLEASE.
I just want to be famous.
I want people to be jealous of me.
Is that so much to ask?

> *(Pause.)*

I already *said* I'd make him move out, okay?

> *(She washes down a lot of Adderall with liquor.)*

What's the point of cutting back?
Once he's gone I won't have any, might as well live it up.
Fine. Leave. What a great friend.
I'm not always afraid of the wrong thing. You are.

14.

(**JULIA** *is at the Home Depot returns counter.*)

Look, sir, I've spent a lot of MONEY here, I bought SIX of these, I installed one on every door of my house, and it's supposed to make a BEEPING noise every time the door opens, it's supposed to BEEP, right? And this morning I'm watching TV and my ex-boyfriend comes WANDERING in from my backyard, and suddenly he's looming over me like a giant stork, and I'm screaming my head off 'cause I didn't know he came in 'cause THERE WAS NO FUCKING BEEP.

I know you don't manufacture these, you just sell them, you get paid like – fucking nothing, it's just – I already owe Shane six thousand dollars, and then I spend five hundred dollars on these fucking alarms that don't work, and – and a restraining order? That's a piece of paper. People wipe their asses with pieces of paper. This is a piece of paper, does this scare you? DOES THIS SCARE YOU? No.

And there are these birds that eat nothing but feces and garbage, and their heads are covered in elephant blood 'cause they stick their whole head inside the carcass –

– Are you calling security?

15.

*(**JULIA** is at home filming herself for YouTube, late at night.)*

What's up guys it's Julia I'm Pretty as Fuck!

So, I know it's been a while. I've lost like – five thousand of you, but whatever, to you guys who stuck around – thank you.

I'm gonna do something a little unusual tonight. I thought I'd do a Q and A. Over the last couple weeks you guys have asked me a lot of questions in the comments. I don't normally like questions, I don't like answering questions, but...I can't sleep, so – you're welcome!

"Dear Julia, my sisters and I love your show! We were wondering, how do you stay so skinny even though you're so old?"

Amphetamines. That was an easy one.

"Omg haha you crazy bitch did you forget to remove yesterday's makeup and then put new makeup over the old?"

...Guilty as charged.

"Hey, just started watching, why does she keep talking about birds?"

Because they're everywhere, and they eat feces, and people, and they hate me.

"Girl, do you ever take out the garbage? Your place is gross."

Okay. I'm not *Martha Stewart* here, I don't know what everyone expects –

(She hears something and stands up.)

Um. Okay. I've been trying to ignore, but that was definitely –

There's someone in my yard. For real this time.

No. Nope. Uh-uh. No more.

I am so fucking sick of this shit!

I'm gonna post this. If I don't come back...I'm dead.

(She turns off the video and searches her home.)

Weapon...weapon...weapon...

(She finds Shane's toolbox and pulls out a hammer. Blackout.)

16.

(Lights up on the mess of Julia's home: makeup, clothes, Diet Cokes, water bottles, toys, food wrappers, plastic bags, pill bottles, bras, Virginia Slims, hair-styling equipment, used makeup remover wipes, Kleenex with lipstick blots, a Home Depot bag, a stack of plates, etc.)

(A large, horrifying bird enters.)

*(**JULIA** faces the bird.)*

Get the fuck out of my yard.

(She lifts the hammer.)

(Blackout.)

(It starts to rain.)

17.

> (**JULIA** *is filming herself for YouTube.*)
>
> (*She is wet, bloody, and her makeup is streaking down her face.*)

Have I ever showed you guys how I take my makeup off?
Probably not.
The only person who's seen me without makeup in the last ten years is my ex-husband.
Does that seem sweet?
It's not.
I'm gonna use Pearlessence Micellar Cleansing Water Facial –
You know what?
It's basically a wet rag.
And I wipe it all over my face.
That's it.
There's nothing to teach.

> (*She uses the wipe to remove all of her makeup. She looks at the wipe.*)

All gone.
It's been great, guys.
But I'm done.

> (*She turns off her camera.*)
>
> (*She sits in shock for a moment.*)
>
> (*She grabs her pill bottle, is about to open it – then throws it across the room.*)
>
> (*She dials her phone.*)

Danny? I did something bad.

18.

*(**DANNY** comes onstage wearing gloves and holding garbage bags. He cleans up Julia's mess. There's blood. It's gory.)*

(He exits.)

(The sound of a chainsaw.)

19.

>(**JULIA** *is at home on the phone, early morning.*)

Did it go okay at the strip mall?
I can buy more garbage bags.
I figure tonight we gotta take care of the rest.
It's wrapped in a plastic bag in my freezer.
I love you.
See you soon.

>(*She looks up.*)

What are you doing up so early Sammy?
Shane's not here, honey.
Well…he went on a trip…to Mexico.
I'm not sure when he's coming back.
But you know who's coming over later?
Daddy.

20.

(JULIA and DANNY are behind Peaches. It's raining.)

JULIA. Imagine a basketball...

DANNY. Not heavy enough...

JULIA. A basketball full of sand. It's wrapped in plastic bags. Monsoon season, it's pouring, there's a flash flood in the ravine behind the strip club.

DANNY. A dry ditch is now a raging river.

JULIA. It's dark, but there's flashes of pink and red from the neon sign. You hold it. You feel its weight. Take it in so you can forget it forever. Then – toss.

DANNY. It arcs in slow motion – Stop-animation –

JULIA. Like a peach.

DANNY. Like a grape.

JULIA. Pink. Peach. Red.

DANNY. Hold at red.

JULIA. Splash.

JULIA & DANNY. Gone.

End of Play

www.ingramcontent.com/pod-product-compliance
Lightning Source LLC
Chambersburg PA
CBHW051412290426
44108CB00015B/2254